Open Letter

Open Letter

On Blasphemy, Islamophobia, and the True Enemies of Free Expression

Originally published in France as

Lettre aux escrocs de l'islamophobie qui font le jeu des racistes

Charb

Little, Brown and Company

New York Boston London

Little, Brown and Company
Hachette Book Group
1290 Avenue of the Americas, New York, NY 10104
littlebrown.com

First English language edition, January 2016
Originally published in France by Les Échappés as *Lettre aux escrocs de
l'islamophobie qui font le jeu des racistes,* April 2015

Little, Brown and Company is a division of Hachette Book Group, Inc. The
Little, Brown name and logo are trademarks of Hachette Book Group, Inc.

The publisher is not responsible for websites (or their content) that are not
owned by the publisher.

ISBN 978-0-316-31133-5
Library of Congress Control Number: 2015955994

10 9 8 7 6 5 4 3 2

Book design by Sean Ford

Printed in the United States of America

Contents

Contents

Foreword

by Adam Gopnik

I read *Charlie Hebdo* for the first time on early sojourns in France, in the 1970s. I am probably a bit of a coward when it comes to comedy—I probably like it sweeter than I should—but I am at least an instinctive pluralist: I really like there to be things in the world, and on the newsstand, that I don't like. *Charlie Hebdo* was not to my taste, but on subsequent, much longer sojourns in France I was always glad to see it persisting; it spoke of an older, rawer French tradition that I could appreciate even if I didn't much care for it. Crude, scabrous, explicit, sacrilegious—its cartooning lacked the charm of the *bande dessinée*. But France is an uptight country that needs the relaxation of the truly, weirdly unfastened—Rabelais could only be French, exactly because the refined needs the raw.

As time passed, I went on to graduate school, and the

history of caricature and cartooning became my academic specialty. And so I began to have a greater appreciation of the ancient roots and impious nobility of the magazine. The *Charlie* cartoonists worked, I realized, in a peculiarly French and savage tradition, born in a long nineteenth-century guerrilla war between republicans and the Church and the monarchy, which had long ago become vestigial everywhere else. Satirical magazines and "name" cartoonists might survive in London and other European capitals, particularly Brussels, but they tend to be artier in touch and more media-centric in concern. *Charlie Hebdo* was a satirical journal of a kind found almost solely in France. In those years, I would go to the flea markets to find and buy old copies of the great caricature magazines of the late nineteenth and early twentieth centuries—*Le Rire* and *La Petite Assiette*—and realized that *Charlie Hebdo* was the last flower, or gasp, of this great tradition. Not at all "meta" or "ironic," like *The Onion,* nor a place for political gossip, like the Parisian weekly *Le Canard Enchaîné* or London's *Private Eye,* it kept alive this French nineteenth-century tradition of direct, high-spirited, and extremely offensive caricature, the very tradition begun by now legendary caricaturist Honoré Daumier, or his editor Charles Philipon, who was put on trial in 1831 for drawing the head of King Louis-Philippe as a pear.

Philipon's famous faux-naïf demonstration of the

process of caricature still brings home the almost primitive kind of image-magic that clings to the act of cartooning. At what point was he guilty? Philipon demanded to know, since the King's head *was* pear-shaped. How could merely simplifying it to its outline be viewed as an attack on the King? The even coarser and more scabrous cartoons that marked the covers of *Charlie Hebdo*—and which took in Jesus and Moses, along with Mohammed; angry rabbis and ranting bishops, along with imams—were the last, well, fruit of that tradition. This, for a doubtless too pedantic eye, was one of the things that made *Charlie* matter; distinguishing French culture from our own modernized one.

The *Charlie* cartoonists were, always, radically democratic and egalitarian in their views, with their one passionate dislike being, simply, the hypocrisies of organized religion. No group has ever been more *"minoritaire"*—more marginalized or on the outs with the political establishment, more vitriolic in its mockery of power, more courageous in opposing people of far greater influence and power than a band of guerrilla cartoonists could ever claim to be. Like their great predecessors, they were always punching up at idols and authorities—and no one in France was more relentlessly, courageously contemptuous of the right-wing Le Pens, *père* et *fille*. In the many years I spent in France, the bracing pleasure of seeing some bit of pious nonsense—from the left sometimes, though more often from the far right—blown apart in an image was the chief pleasure of reading *Charlie Hebdo.*

That perhaps-too-cultured response became nugatory one January morning in 2015, when two Islamic fundamentalist terrorists entered the offices of *Charlie Hebdo,* inadequately guarded by the French police, and with cold-blooded cruelty murdered eight staffers as well as a policeman. (They then murdered a helpless Muslim policeman lying wounded on the street outside.) And yet this terrorist atrocity left an honest observer with a somewhat uneasily divided conscience: on the one hand, the *Charlie* cartoonists were undoubtedly martyrs to free speech, freedom of expression, and the essential fight against fundamentalisms of all kind. On the other... well, a small irreverent smile came to the lips at the thought of the flag being lowered, as it was throughout France, for these anarchist mischief-makers, and they would surely have roared at the irony of their being solemnly mourned and marched for by former president Nicolas Sarkozy and current president François Hollande. (The cartoonists didn't just mock those men's politics; they regularly amplified their sexual appetites and diminished their sexual appurtenances.)

To resolve these two sides of *Charlie*—the heroic martyrs, the ongoing mockers; the men of the world, the frightened marginalized victims—is the purpose of the book you hold now. In it the great *Charlie* cartoonist and editor Charb—exasperated, logical, intelligent, above all humane—takes apart all the noxious myths that had circulated about *Charlie Hebdo* in the past and that have accumulated in the year since the killings; the myth of its "Islamophobia," for instance. Charb explicates the difference between mockery and assault in a rational manner made almost unbearably poignant by the cost he and his friends would pay to the wholly irrational.

Throughout, his arguments have a simple distinction at their core—that criticizing an ideology, including a religious ideology, however vociferously, is different from inducing hatred of a people or persons. There is a huge space between an insult and a threat, and it isn't actually that hard to tell one from the other. In an open society, we all have to put up with insults. Islam, an ideology like any other—as is Communism or Liberalism or Judaism—can be criticized and mocked like any other. Charb reminds us that "the fashion of adding '-phobia' to the end of every other word is perfectly ludicrous. 'Homophobia' and 'negrophobia' are used to describe the hatred people may feel not toward an ideology or a religion, but toward human beings, pure and simple."

In other words, saying that someone's religion is ridiculous is different—discernably, measurably, significantly different—from saying that some group should be exterminated. Mocking your prophet is not at all like threatening your person. Blasphemy is ridicule directed at an ideology; hate speech encourages violence directed at individuals. Judeophobia—the mockery of the religion of Moses of the kind that Voltaire engaged in at length—ought to be protected, no matter who engages in it, just as *South Park*'s mockery of Mormonism should. But Jews and Mormons must not be threatened, either in the practice of their faith or in their confidence in their own continued well-being. Blasphemy is just the fanatic's name for criticism. Charb writes, wisely:

> A believer can blaspheme only to the extent that the idea of blasphemy holds any meaning for him. A nonbeliever, no matter how hard he tries, *cannot* blaspheme. God is sacred only to those who believe in him. If you wish to insult or offend God, you have to be sure that he exists. The strategy used by minority group activists masquerading as anti-racists is to pass off blasphemy as Islamophobia and Islamophobia as racism.

The crucial distinction we must defend is between acts of imagination and acts of violence. The imagination sees and draws and describes many things—pornographic, erotic, satiric, and blasphemous—that are uncomfortable or ugly. But they are not actually happening. The imagination is a place where hypotheses and conditionals rule, and where part of the fun, and most of the point, lies in saying the unsayable in order to test the truths of what's most often said. An assault on an ideology is not merely different from a threat made to a person; it is the opposite of a threat made to a person. The whole end of liberal civilization is to substitute the criticism of ideas for assaults on people. The idea that we should be free to do our work and offer our views without extending a frightened veto to those who threaten to harm us if we do isn't just part of what we mean by free expression. It's what free expression is. The social contract at the heart of liberalism is simple: in exchange for the freedom to be as insulting as you want about other people's ideas, you have to give up the possibility of assaulting other people's persons.

Faith is not the enemy. Fanaticism is the enemy. It always is. But only a fool would deny that faith has been the seedbed of fanaticism in mankind's long and sorry struggle for the light. As much as at times we need to seek "solidarity" among unlike groups, we also need to "desolidarize," to "unsolidarize"—to put the people we know before the abstract categories we imagine. Come to think of it, making people, with all their flaws, fully visible while leaving generalized types alone is exactly what the caricaturist has always done for us. It's his special form of bravery.

Note from the publisher

This text was finalized on January 5, 2015, two days before the terrorist attack on *Charlie Hebdo* in which Charb was killed.

If you think criticizing religion is an expression of racism,

If you think "Islam" is the name of a people,

If you think it's okay to make fun of everything except what is sacred to you,

If you think sending blasphemers to jail will get you into heaven,

If you think humor is incompatible with Islam,

If you think a cartoon is more dangerous than an American drone,

If you think Muslims have no sense of humor or irony,

If you think leftist atheists are playing into the hands of reactionaries and xenophobes,

If you think someone with Muslim parents must also be Muslim,

If you think you know how many Muslims there are in France,

If you think it is important to identify citizens by their religion,

If you think popularizing the concept of Islamophobia is the best way to defend Islam,

If you think defending Islam is the best way to defend Muslims,

If you think the Koran forbids drawing the prophet Muhammad,

If you think a caricature of a jihadist looking ridiculous is an insult to Islam,

If you think that when right-wing crazies attack an Arab they are really attacking Islam,

If you think every ethnic group should have its own anti-racism association,

If you think Islamophobia is the counterpart of anti-Semitism,

If you think the Zionists who run the world have paid a stooge to write this book,

Well, happy reading, because this letter is for you.

Islamophobia is the new racism

Let's face it—the term "Islamophobia" is poorly chosen if it's meant to describe the hatred felt by a few morons for Muslims. And it's not just poorly chosen, but dangerous.

If we look at it from a purely etymological perspective, "Islamophobia" should mean "fear of Islam." But the inventors, promoters, and users of the word deploy it to denounce hatred of Muslims. I find it odd that "Muslimophobia," or the broader term "racism," has not gained ground over "Islamophobia." Either of those would be on a firmer footing, semantically speaking. So why has "Islamophobia" won the day?

Out of ignorance, laziness, and error, for some, but also because many of those who militate against Islamophobia do so not to defend Muslims as individuals, but to defend the religion of the prophet Muhammad.

Racism has existed in all countries ever since the invention of the scapegoat. There will probably always be racists. The solution is not to paw through the minds of every citizen, searching for the least little ember of racism, but to prevent racists from putting their nauseating ideas into words, from claiming their "right" to be racists, to express their hatred.

In France, racist speech was largely set free by Sarkozy[1] and the issue he made of national identity. When the highest authority of the state stands up in front of assholes and bastards and tells them, "Let 'er rip, boys," what do you think the assholes and bastards are going to do? They're going to start saying

---

1   Nicolas Sarkozy (born 1955), President of France from 2007 to 2012

publicly what, up till then, they had limited themselves to belching out at the drunken conclusion of family dinners. Racist speech, which our institutions, politicians, and intellectuals had succeeded in confining to the zone between the xenophobe's teeth and his kitchen door, made its way out into the street, flooded the media, and further befouled the plumbing of social networks.

Yes, we are witnessing a renaissance of racist outbursts, yet the term "racism" is only used timidly these days. The term "racism" is quite simply in the process of being superseded by "Islamophobia."

When a veiled woman is harassed and assaulted because she is veiled in the Muslim fashion (the elusive aggressor generally being described as a skinhead), the anti-Islamophobe champions the victim as a representative of Islam. Not because she is a citizen who happens to have been singled out by a fascist for her beliefs. For her champion, the sin lies in the fact that she has been attacked not as a citizen who has the right to dress as she likes, but as a Muslim woman. The real victim is Islam. God has thus been placed well above his believer, but when the latter is harmed, God is the intended target. This is what the anti-Islamophobic activist finds truly unacceptable.

And that's why anti-Islamophobes have not chosen to call themselves "anti-Muslimophobes." They consider the Muslims they defend to be merely the instruments of God.

It's gotten to the point where you might get the impression that foreigners or citizens of foreign extraction are assaulted in France solely for being Muslims. Victims of racism who are of Indian, Asian, Roma, black African, or Caribbean descent may soon need to find themselves a religion if they wish to be protected.

Minority pressure group activists who seek to impose the concept of "Islamophobia" on judicial and political authorities have only one goal: to persuade the victims of racism to proclaim themselves Muslim. Forgive me, but the fact that racists may also be Islamophobic is essentially incidental. They are racists first, and merely use Islam to target their intended victim: the foreigner or person of foreign extraction. By taking only the racist's Islamophobia into account, we minimize the danger of his racism. Yesterday's anti-racism activist is turning into the salesman of a highly specialized commodity: a niche form of discrimination. The fight against racism is a fight against all forms of racism; but what is the fight against Islamophobia against? Is it against criticizing a religion or against abhorring its practitioners because they are of foreign descent? Racists have a field day when we debate whether it is racist to say the Koran is a useless rag. If tomorrow the Muslims of France were to convert to Catholicism or renounce all religion, it wouldn't make the least bit of difference to the racists—they would continue to hold these foreigners or French citizens of foreign descent responsible for every affliction.

Okay, so Mouloud and Gérard are Muslims. Mouloud is of North African extraction and comes from a Muslim family; Gérard is of European origin and comes from a Catholic family. Gérard has converted to Islam. Both are trying to rent the same apartment. Assuming they have similar incomes, which of the two Muslims is more likely to get the apartment? The Arab-looking fellow or the white guy? It's not the Muslim who will be turned away; it's the Arab. The fact that the Arab bears no outward sign of belonging to the Muslim faith changes nothing. Yet what does the anti-Islamophobia activist do? He charges religious discrimination instead of decrying racism.

I recall here the relevant section of the Penal Code:

Discrimination comprises any distinction applied between natural persons by reason of their origin, sex, family situation, pregnancy, physical appearance or patronymic, place of residence, state of health, handicap, genetic characteristics, sexual morals or orientation, age, political opinions, union activities, or their membership or non-membership, true or supposed, of a given ethnic group, nation, race or religion.[2]

---

2   Article 225-1, http://www.legifrance.gouv.fr

Social discrimination, while the subject of much less debate than religious discrimination because it is manifested more insidiously and discreetly, is nevertheless far more predominant in France. Managers choose their future employees less on the basis of their religious membership, true or supposed, than, for instance, on their place of residence. Between the Mouloud who lives in upscale Neuilly-sur-Seine and the Mouloud who lives in the down-at-heel *banlieue* of Argenteuil, which of the two, assuming they are of equal competence, is more likely to get the job? Yet who ever talks about this kind of discrimination? People are massively discriminated against based on their social class, but since a large proportion of the poor—whom no one wants hanging around their place of work, their neighborhood, or their building—is made up of people of foreign descent and, among these, a great many of Muslim origin, the Islamic activist will claim that the problem is Islamophobia.

Let's take a look at the example of Mouloud and Abdelkader. Both are Muslims, both are of foreign descent, both are darker-skinned than Gérard. Mouloud is flat broke; Abdelkader is a millionaire. Which of the two will be rejected for the apartment? The Muslim Mouloud or the millionaire Abdelkader?

While we may need to reject the terms "Islamophobia" or "Christianophobia," which I will return to later, what about the equally novel concepts of "homophobia" or "negrophobia"? The simple fact is that neither of these terms is ambiguous, even if the fashion of adding "-phobia" to the end of every other word is perfectly ludicrous. "Homophobia" and "negrophobia" are used to describe the hatred people may feel not toward an ideology or a religion, but toward human beings, pure and simple. Homophobia should be condemned not because it implies criticism of homosexuality, but because it expresses hatred of homosexuals. Likewise, when we speak of negrophobia, we are clearly speaking about the hatred that some express against black people, against individuals.

Faith is submission

To believe is, above all, to fear

According to the dictionary, "Islam" means "submission" in Arabic. A Muslim is someone who is *submissive* to God. Why does he submit? Because his God is the best, the brawniest, the nattiest, but most of all because, if he says anything to the contrary, he will burn in hell until well after the end of the world. The believer is thus encouraged not to screw around with God under penalty of something worse than death for all eternity. So shouldn't we prosecute all the imams, rabbis, and priests who exhort their flocks to fear the Lord? Do these devoted servants of their Lord not contribute to a sort of theophobia?

It's easy to see how a certain kind of impressionable fuckwit believer, having attended the weekly sermon, might head home in a cold sweat, convinced his every movement is under divine scrutiny. God is a super-surveillance camera that no one seriously objects to. And yet, it was installed without input from a single elected official or voter. But I digress.

One day, just for fun, I will have to publish a collection of all the hate mail I've received at *Charlie Hebdo* from Catholic fascists and Muslim fascists. The main argument against blasphemy is just plain stupid: after our death, God will really stick it to us. Wouldn't it be perfectly normal for certain sensitive souls to develop a phobia of religions that threaten them? A phobia of God?

By these lights, the main Islamophobes are the believers themselves. They're shitting themselves at the thought that their vengeful God will punish them for the least slip-up.

Being afraid is a right

Being afraid of Islam is no doubt moronic, absurd, and plenty of other things as well, but it's not a crime. Likewise, you can demonstrate your fear of Christianity or Judaism without disturbing a judge and setting the whole legal system in motion. In any case, an adherent himself may well have a phobia of other religions. He has been taught that his religion is the best of all—no, not the best, the only True One! By declaring that the texts he holds sacred tell the truth, he implies that the others tell fibs. It's easy to imagine him terrified by the prospect of mass conversions to the false religion. Or, more precisely, of a mass exodus of the clientele to the competition. There's nothing surprising about a Catholic being Islamophobic or a Muslim being Cathophobic—that is precisely what their religious shepherds ask them to be. Disapproval of the other guy's religion is the daily bread of clerics of all creeds, and nobody seems to be bothered by it. Priests, imams, and rabbis have the right to be Islamophobic, Judeophobic, or Cathophobic without reprimand.

Let us recall, too, that a religion does not exist without believers. A text becomes sacred and, ultimately, dangerous only when some fanatic decides to take his bedside reading literally. You have to be really gullible to swallow the foundational texts of any of the great religions word for word, and you'd have to be a true psychopath to try to reproduce their teachings at home. In short, the problem is neither the Koran nor the Bible—tiresome, incoherent, and poorly written novels though they may be—but the faithful who read the Koran or the Bible the way you read the assembly instructions for an Ikea bookcase. If you don't do exactly what it says on the paper, the universe will blow the fuck up. If I don't slit the infidel's throat along the dotted line, God will banish me from Club Med when I die.

Take any cookbook, declare everything written in it to be the Truth, and apply it to the letter, for yourself and others, as prescribed in these new Holy Scriptures. The outcome? A bloodbath. Your neighbor cooks gluten-free pancakes because he's allergic? The Holy Book makes no provision for such behavior! Put your blaspheming neighbor to the torch! He butters his pie dish too liberally? Kill! Kill!

You can do the same experiment with any book. Try it out with a Stephen King novel, for a laugh.

All currents of thought may be criticized

"Sacred" texts are sacred only to those who believe in them. While some Muslim and Catholic institutions have been working for years to have the crime of blasphemy recognized and actionable under French law, no one is in danger of going to jail for criticizing such or such religious dogma (except in Alsace-Moselle, which we'll get back to).

A believer can blaspheme only to the extent that the idea of blasphemy holds any meaning for him. A nonbeliever, no matter how hard he tries, *cannot* blaspheme. God is sacred only to those who believe in him. If you wish to insult or offend God, you have to be sure that he exists. The strategy used by minority group activists masquerading as anti-racists is to pass off blasphemy as Islamophobia and Islamophobia as racism.

For example, no communist would ever consider identifying anti-communists as communistophobes, or prosecuting them on the grounds of anti-communist racism. No matter how hard you try to bend reality to your way of thinking, you'll have a hard time convincing anyone that there is such a thing as a communist "race." Likewise, there is no such thing as the Islamic "race." Communism, as a school of thought, is now in the minority in France, regularly attacked or at the very least mercilessly derided by all faithful champions of the triumphant capitalist model. There are not (alas) a billion-plus communists in the world; the Communist Party is not (alas) the second-largest in France; there are (alas) more mosques than Communist Party federations; and no communist who interacts with customers at work is allowed to sport a big fat yellow hammer and sickle on his red T-shirt.

While, unlike the existence of God, it is difficult to deny the existence of Marx, Lenin, or Georges Marchais,[3] it is neither blasphemous, racist, nor communistophobic to cast doubt on the validity of their writings or their speech. In France, a religion is nothing more than a collection of texts, traditions, and customs that it is perfectly legitimate to criticize. Sticking a clown nose on Marx is no more offensive or scandalous than popping the same schnoz on Muhammad.

God is big enough to take care of himself

Frankly, if God exists and is as powerful as his minions claim, we infidels, unbelievers, layfolk, atheists, antitheists, free thinkers, and apostates are in deep shit. We are irremediably damned to the fires of hell.

Which raises the question: Why do believers resort to human justice to punish us when divine justice

---

3   Georges Marchais (1920–1997), General Secretary of the French Communist Party from 1972 to 1994

would do the trick, far more severely than any judge? Exactly who is this God character, who is said to be all-powerful yet needs to hire lawyers to take us to court? Isn't he miffed when someone he had always considered to be a true follower turns to the legal system rather than to prayer? Why would the faithful risk making God look ridiculous by losing a trial on Earth when he is certain to win every trial in heaven? I don't want to quarrel with anyone, but from the believer's perspective, isn't it blasphemy to ask jurists who may themselves be nonbelievers to condemn other nonbelievers in the name of God? Isn't being the lead lawyer on God's defense team just another way of committing the sin of pride? Does God—the creator of the world, this swaggering broad-shouldered guy who toys with our planet the way a driver stopped at a red light toys with his boogers—really need some ambulance chaser to uphold his honor?

By taking blasphemers to court, our minority pressure groups prove only one thing: they don't believe in God.

Or else they are in favor of convicting people twice for the same crime, which is particularly mean-spirited and perverse. They want us to be found guilty and sentenced here in France, and a second time Up There. Or should I say Down There, since it is commonly understood that hell is in the basement and paradise, upstairs.

Believers who want to put a handful of blasphemers through hell on Earth are counterfeiters. How could even the most talented disciple hope to rival God by patching together a pale imitation of the official hell, where the skin of supplicants grows back every time it is flayed? Disneyland would sue anyone who dared to open a park modeled on the original without authorization. It's astonishing that God, who is reputed to be even more of a stickler for the rules than the Disney heirs, does not severely punish those do-it-yourself believers who try to profit from an earthly theme park to which they don't own the rights.

Elitism, condescension, and infantilization

Journalists promoting Islamophobia

The term "Islamophobia" could never have achieved such wild popularity without the—mostly idiotic—complicity of the media. Why were they so eager to co-opt Islamophobia? First out of laziness, then for the novelty of it, and lastly out of commercial interest. Their contribution to popularizing the term "Islamophobia" has never been motivated by the least impulse to combat racism. On the contrary.

To put it simply, any scandal containing the word "Islam" in its headline sells copy. Ever since the attacks of September 11, 2001, the media have placed a fascinating and frightening character at center stage: the Islamist terrorist. Any terrorist can scare the hell out of us, but if you make him Islamist to boot, we all shit ourselves. Fear sells well. Scary Islam sells well. And scary Islam has become the only Islam there is in the eyes of the public at large.

Because the Islam that the media shovel down consumers' throats is by necessity radical and bearded. When the mainstream media present a report on Islam it is very often a caricature, yet it provokes little open protest from the pressure groups that track Islamophobia. So long as they're invited to put in their two cents on the rise of Islamophobia, everybody's happy.

On the other hand, when a cartoon of so-called radical Islam is presented as a genuine and deliberate caricature, the Islamophobia-busters lose their cool. If you want to thrive in the media ecosystem, it's far safer to take on a little newspaper like *Charlie Hebdo* than to attack major television channels and newsmagazines.

•   •   •

Nowadays, when a journalist asks a Muslim to comment on "the rise of Islamophobia," what he's really asking for is commentary on something the media themselves have created. In other words, the reporter helps to amplify the problem and then claims to be surprised that the problem exists and endures. The Muslim leader whom the prime-time anchor has called on to express his opinion of this notorious "rise of Islamophobia" should spit in his eye. He is face-to-face with the guy whose very job is to peddle fear of Islam.

The Muhammad Cartoons

Charlie Hebdo published cartoons of Muhammad long before the scandal of the Danish cartoons.[4] Note that, before the so-called Muhammad cartoons affair,

---

4   On September 30, 2005, the Danish newspaper *Jyllands-Posten,* in an attempt to spark a debate about Islam and self-censorship, published twelve cartoons depicting the prophet Muhammad. The publication gave rise to violent protests around the world.

the artists of *Charlie Hebdo* were known as and considered themselves to be journalistic illustrators. Ever since, they have generally been described as cartoonists.

Without denying the utility of cartoons in reporting current events, satiric caricature is but one element of drawing. There's no shame in it at all, but this one detail highlights the extent to which the cartoons of Muhammad have colored the general public's view of the work done by the artists of *Charlie Hebdo* ever since.

As I said, the Muslim prophet had been depicted in *Charlie Hebdo* long before the aforementioned scandal. No pressure group or reporter had expressed dismay of any kind over these drawings. A few individuals had conveyed their disapproval by letter, nothing more. No demonstrations, no death threats, no attacks. It was only after the denunciation and exploitation of the Danish cartoons by a group of Muslim extremists that caricaturing the prophet of the faithful suddenly became the trigger of media and Islamic hysteria. Media first, Islamic later. In 2006, when *Charlie Hebdo* reaffirmed an artist's right to caricature religious terrorism by republishing the Danish cartoons of Muhammad, the media turned their cameras on our satirical paper. *Charlie Hebdo* became yet another potential target for the wrath of God's wingnuts. The publication of the cartoons generated a tsunami of publicity, not because they were especially shocking, but because they could only be shocking, given how they were exploited to provoke outrage abroad.

The cartoon showing Muhammad wearing a turban in the form of a bomb is the best known among them. While not everyone interpreted it in the same way, it was at least open to interpretation by all, since it did not include text. Its detractors decided to read it as an insult to all Muslims.

To give the prophet of the faithful a bomb for a hat was to suggest that all his followers were terrorists. Another interpretation was possible, but it did not interest the media as much since it was not inflammatory, and therefore didn't sell copy. Showing Muhammad in a bomb-hat could have been a way of condemning the exploitation of religion by terrorists. The cartoon was saying, "This is what terrorists have done to Islam. This is how the terrorists who claim to follow the prophet see him."

It was because the media had decided that the reissue of the Muhammad cartoons could only unleash the fury of Muslims that it unleashed the ire of a few Muslim organizations. For some, their anger was just for show. Once they found themselves hemmed in by microphones and cameras, with reporters demanding their views on the blasphemous nature of the cartoons, the spokespersons of these pressure groups had no choice but to react. They had to prove to the most riled-up believers that they were true defenders of the faith.

The most radical Muslims compensate for their low numbers with intense, militant activism. Everyone falls for it, Muslim organizations and journalists alike. Because they have the biggest mouths, they become Islam—the real Islam. The truth is that there are few Muslims who observe all their religious obligations. And among those, the majority are not involved in religious groups, moderate or otherwise. That's totally understandable. They don't need someone telling them how they ought to believe.

Islam may very well be the second most practiced

religion in France, but that doesn't mean that all immigrants or children of immigrants from predominantly Muslim countries are Muslims themselves. I recall that in 2010, according to a report issued by the National Institute of Demographic Studies and the National Institute of Statistics and Economic Studies, 2.1 million persons in France called themselves Muslims, while 11.5 million called themselves Catholics and 125,000 called themselves Jews. These figures have never been cited by minority activists, who continue to claim—depending on their mood, which way the wind blows, or their own interests—that there are six, eight, ten, or even thirteen million Muslims in France!

Thankfully, faith is not transmitted genetically, as minority pressure groups and the far right would like to have us believe. But if your parents are Muslims, or assumed to be so on the basis of their origins, you will be considered a Muslim by the pressure groups and the reactionaries. Reporters, who need to inflate the "alarming" figures, are only too happy for a few minority-group leaders in search of notoriety and power to serve up those numbers on a platter.

•   •   •

Ever since the Muhammad cartoons affair and the no-torious trial that followed, *Charlie Hebdo* has been under almost continuous media surveillance. Only dare to publish a cover representing the prophet or even someone who might be mistaken for him, and they're off! The drawing in question is described as "yet another provocation from *Charlie Hebdo.*" And when the TV says it's a provocation, there's always some group of morons out there ready to consider themselves provoked. If the press calls it a scandal, someone out there will be scandalized.

Who are these Islamophobes? They're the ones who claim that Muslims are stupid enough to get bent out of shape over some ridiculous drawing. A drawing that was widely viewable only because it was broadcast on every channel. Islamophobia is a market not only for those who make a profession of condemning it, but also for the press that promotes it.

Politics promoting Islamophobia

Reporters are not the only ones who see Muslims where they ought to see citizens. Too many politicians also sell the Republic short by cozying up to so-called believers instead of to citizens. Special-interest advocacy, which everyone condemns in speech, is encouraged in deed.

To cite just one example—an egregious one, given that it stars a socialist President of the Republic—on February 18, 2014, François Hollande visited the Grand Mosque of Paris to inaugurate a memorial honoring Muslim soldiers who died for France from 1914 to 1918. We can understand the President drooling over the idea of a Muslim electorate, since the socialists are convinced that such a thing exists—that is, that most Muslims cast their votes not on the basis of candidates' political ideas, but based on the amount of affection these candidates lavish on Muslims. This concept assumes that Muslims, as prisoners of their Muslim identities, can think only in their capacity as Muslims. You'd have to take Muslims for nitwits to believe such a thing. Or for overcooked spaghetti. The socialists think that if you plunge your fork into a bowl of Muslims and twist, you'll pull out the entire bowlful. They're one solid mass. Yet again, Muslims are considered first as Muslims before being considered as citizens. Yet that, somehow, is not Islamophobia.

It's perfectly natural for Muslim leaders to pay homage to Muslims killed in the First World War. But it's absurd for a President of the Republic to pay homage to Muslims "who died for France." These natives—the colonized and enslaved who, for the most part, were rounded up and enlisted by force—did not die for France in their capacity as Muslims. They died in their capacity as low-cost cannon fodder. And if they did die for France, it wasn't by choice. They died because of France; they died defending a country that had stolen their own. Hollande honored them as heroes, but they were, above all, victims. Before them, German bullets; behind them, French bayonets.

Among the 100,000 native colonial casualties of the Great War who are purported to have been Muslims, it would be astonishing to find even one who fought to defend the values of Islam. Can anyone imagine Muslim poilus engaging in jihad on France's behalf? Socialist comrades, don't mistake yesterday's colonials for today's imbeciles. Let the Republic raise a monument to the colonial peoples it led to slaughter rather than dream up Muslim fighters who died for France! How could Hollande not see the grotesque irony of the situation? Having kowtowed to the memory of Muslim soldiers, why not in the future kowtow to the memory of atheist soldiers, homosexual soldiers, vegetarian soldiers, albino soldiers, freemason soldiers, Orthodox Christian soldiers, Sephardic Jewish soldiers, pacifist soldiers, soldiers who played the ponies, soldiers who believed that the Sun revolves around the Earth...?

France is a salami that the Socialist Party has the annoying tendency of slicing up into special-interest groups. And it does so not out of respect for these purported groups, but out of political interest. Too many cultural associations assign the official "Muslim" label to immigrants who ask nothing more than to be treated as citizens—either because they are not Muslims, or because they can practice their faith without the support of dubiously representative associations.

It is astounding to see Hollande suck up to the shopkeepers of faith. Needless to say, not a single journalist or activist in the struggle against Islamophobia criticized the President's gesture. Ultimately, what all of them really want is for Muslims to be seen exclusively as Muslims.

The Socialist Party has been promising to give foreigners the right to vote for over thirty years. François Hollande made it a campaign promise. Once elected, the President declared several times that he was in favor of it. But he waited until December 15, 2014, on the occasion of the inauguration of the Museum of the History of Immigration, and only *after* the Senate had swung back to the right, to deplore the fact that the opposition was against such a reform. Allowing non-EU foreigners to vote in local elections[5] requires a constitutional amendment that must be approved by three-fifths of the Parliament. Did François Hollande launch a national debate on the issue? No. He feels it is less politically risky to pay homage to "Mus-

---

5   Citizens of EU countries may vote in local elections in any EU member state.

lims" who died for France than to grant a legitimate right to immigrants who participate in the daily life of the country.

An elite who infantilizes Muslims in the name of the struggle against Islamophobia

But if the artists of *Charlie Hebdo* understand that their cartoons may be exploited by the media, the hucksters of Islamophobia, the Muslim extreme right, or the nationalist extreme right, why do they insist on caricaturing Muhammad and depicting the "sacred" symbols of Islam?

Quite simply because *Charlie Hebdo*'s cartoons do not target Muslims as a whole. But what happens when, following overexposure in the media, Muslims as a whole gain access to the drawings? The artists of *Charlie Hebdo* believe that not all Muslims are intolerant of a cheeky sense of humor. What twisted theory makes humor less compatible with Islam than with any other religion? Asserting that Islam is not compatible with humor is as absurd as claiming that Islam is not compatible with democracy or secular governance.

If we suggest that it is okay to make fun of everything except certain aspects of Islam because Muslims are much more sensitive than the rest of the population, isn't that discrimination? Shouldn't we treat the second-largest religion of the world, the purported second religion in France, exactly as we treat the first? It's time to put an end to the revolting paternalism of the white, middle-class, "leftist" intellectual trying to coexist with these "poor, subliterate wretches." "*I'm* educated; obviously I get that *Charlie Hebdo* is a humor newspaper because, first, I'm very intelligent, and second, it's my culture. But you—well, you haven't quite mastered nuanced thinking yet, so I'll express my solidarity by fulminating against Islamophobic cartoons and pretending not to understand them. I will lower myself to your level to show you that I like you. And if I need to convert to Islam to get even closer to you, I'll do it!" These pathetic demagogues just have a ravenous need for recognition and a formidable domination fantasy to fulfill.

Heroes in the struggle against *Charlie Hebdo's* so-called Islamophobia

Lawsuits and the clowns who file them

Monsieur Zaoui Saada tops the list. He may not be the best known of our detractors, but he is certainly the most pugnacious. He is the leader (both President and Secretary-General) of the United Arab Organization, which is itself a "branch" of the Algerian Democratic Rally for Peace and Progress. Yup, all that.

He made his name in 2006 by suing *Charlie Hebdo* for the crime of "incitement to discrimination, hatred or violence toward a group of persons by reason of their origins, ethnicity or religion, and incitement to crimes and misdemeanors." Take a deep breath—there's more. He also sued us for "insult to the memory of the Prophet Muhammad, and direct insult to the Muslim community." These lawsuits were an explicit response to the publication of the Danish Muhammad cartoons. He sought €200,000 for each of his organizations, and €20,000 for himself by reason of "moral wrong." It's true that, given his personal intimacy with the Prophet, he must surely have been more deeply affected than any other Muslim by the unacceptable violence of a dozen humorous cartoons. Mr. Zaoui Saada was awarded nothing, other than a few lines in the press.

In December 2012, Mr. Zaoui Saada again drew attention to himself by suing *Charlie Hebdo* for publishing, in its September 19 issue of that year, several drawings mocking both *Innocence of Muslims,* an anti-Islam "film" available online, and the over-the-top response of a few Muslims to that pathetic turkey. Under the title "Intouchables 2," the cover art of that issue of *Charlie* shows a Muslim in a wheelchair being pushed by an Orthodox Jew.[6] This time, Mr. Zaoui Saada's two organizations and Mr. Saada in his own right sought a total of €782,000. Every drawing that seemed to portray the Prophet, explicitly or otherwise—including one making fun of the director of the anti-Islam movie—was targeted for prosecution. Even an absurdist cartoon of an enraged Salafist pointing at Bugs Bunny and exclaiming: "Another insulting representation of our Prophet!" Thanks to the publicity we reaped from the professionally indignant, we had to go to a second printing of that issue, which was released on a Friday. Yes, the Muslim day of rest. Believe it or not, Mr. Saada used that as another pretext to justify his lawsuits.

On trial day, Mr. Saada, represented by his lawyer, did not appear in Trial Chamber 17 of the Paris Magistrate's Court. We were given to understand that Mr. Saada, a "management consultant" in the civilian world, was detained elsewhere. In prison, to be precise. Accused of attempted extortion against a retired com-

---

6   *The Intouchables* (2011) is a French film in which a wealthy paraplegic is tended by a young man of color from the projects.

pany director from the town of Jonzac, in the department of Charente-Maritime, Mr. Saada found himself in provisional custody. Mr. Saada's lawyer did not even bother showing up to the second hearing in Chamber 11. One can only imagine the disappointment of the billions of Muslims offended by the *Charlie Hebdo* cartoons, whom Mr. Saada claimed to represent.

Another notable avenger against *Charlie Hebdo* was the renowned Karim Achoui. An attorney disbarred in 2012, he was frequently referred to as an "underworld lawyer" by a mainstream press that often forgets that even mobsters enjoy the right to a defense. Deprived of his primary source of revenue, Karim Achoui was a latecomer to the cause of defending Islam. In 2013, he founded the Muslim Legal Defense League, an organization dedicated to fighting Islamophobia. He claimed at the time that hundreds of jurists and attorneys had signed on to his struggle. He even boasted of having recruited a former government minister, Roland Dumas, although the latter never publicly confirmed his involvement.

Immediately after establishing his organization, of which he appeared to be the sole representative, he announced his intention to sue *Charlie Hebdo* for incitement to racial hatred. On August 9, 2013, on *Marianne* magazine's website, Achoui described his action as "a community struggle for individual freedoms."

His target was the front page of the July 10, 2013, issue of *Charlie Hebdo,* drawn by Riss. The drawing depicted the violence perpetrated by the Egyptian army against the Muslim Brotherhood. It showed an Islamist vainly trying to use a Koran to shield himself against gunfire. The text said, "The Koran is a piece of shit—it doesn't stop bullets." Faced with physical violence and the prospect of death, the believer who had once sought to impose his religious vision on an entire nation comes to the tragic understanding that God is not as powerful as he'd thought. Apparently, that was not how Mr. Achoui chose to interpret it. The only thing he saw was "The Koran is a piece of shit," and he cited that phrase alone, deliberately removed from its context and interpreted literally, as the basis for his lawsuit. A good soldier in the fight against Islamophobia is sometimes forced to dumb it down.

As director of publication for *Charlie Hebdo,* I received two summonses for the same drawing from two different legal jurisdictions and for two separate complaints. I was charged by the Paris Municipal Court with incitement to hatred on the basis of religious affiliation, and by the Strasbourg Magistrate's Court for blasphemy. Provincial law in Alsace and Moselle indeed allows plaintiffs to sue citizens for blasphemy in the departments of Bas-Rhin, Haut-Rhin, and Moselle. Can a "racist" cartoon in Paris constitute blasphemy in Strasbourg? In theory, it can. And in practice, too.

Article 166 of the local penal code lays it out: "Anyone who disturbs the peace by using indecent language to blaspheme against God in public, or publicly insults a Christian denomination or religious community established on Confederation territory and recognized as a corporate body, or the institutions or rituals of these denominations, or who, in a church or other place consecrated to religious assembly, commits insulting or abusive acts, shall be punished by a maximum of three years' imprisonment."

How is such a thing possible in a secular republic?

In 1905, Alsace-Moselle was exempt from the law establishing the separation of church and state because the territory was German at the time. In 1919, when France recovered Alsace-Moselle, which had been annexed by Germany under Bismarck in 1871, nothing was done to adapt local legislation to French law. The salaries of priests, pastors, and rabbis are paid by the state, and the maintenance of Catholic, Protestant, and Jewish facilities is underwritten by local governments. Moreover, "religious instruction" at school is compulsory.

Karim Achoui took good note of the fact that Islam was not among the religions recognized under Alsace-Moselle law, which had gone unamended since 1871. It would be logical for Islam, supposedly the second religion of France, to be treated on an equal footing as Catholicism, Protestantism, and Judaism under Alsace-Moselle law. By suing *Charlie Hebdo* in Strasbourg, Karim Achoui's principal aim was not to prosecute the newspaper but to highlight the incoherence of local law. Karim Achoui was open about his readiness to use the suit against *Charlie Hebdo,* which he knew to be lost from the outset, in order to raise an application before the Constitutional Council for a preliminary ruling on the conformity of a legislative provision with the Constitution. His goal, announced on the sectarian website Oumma.com, was to "reform and revise the law of 1905," which, according to him, was "an insult to the 5 or 10 million Muslims of France." Since neither the provincial law of Alsace-Moselle nor the law on the separation of church and state recognize the existence of Muslims, a new law therefore had to be considered that would take the faith of these millions of believers into account. At least that's how I understood it.

We never had the chance to argue this issue with the Muslim Legal Defense League before the bench, either in Paris or in Strasbourg, because that assemblage of eminent lawyers never managed to file the necessary paperwork with the courts in question, or even to respond to the judges' summonses. Too bad. Our lawyer would have enjoyed having his own opportunity to point out the absurdity of the sectarian laws of Alsace-Moselle and to call for their repeal. Karim Achoui had kicked up a lot of fuss for nothing. At least he managed to get himself voted 2013 "Person of the Year" by the readers of Oumma.com!

Sadly, there's more percentage in believing in God than in believing in Karim Achoui. The last time I visited the Muslim Legal Defense League's website it was still under construction. The League is apparently no more skilled at IT than it is at the law. Its Facebook page is nothing more than one big infomercial to the glory of a disbarred lawyer.

Organizations misdirecting their indignation

What can I say about those who signed a petition launched the day after the arson attack on *Charlie Hebdo*'s offices, following the publication of the renowned issue "Charia Hebdo"? The petition was headlined "In defense of freedom of expression and against support for *Charlie Hebdo!*" The 2011 attack on *Charlie* had received massive media coverage and been broadly condemned, including by Marine Le Pen[7] (which, thankfully, did not stop her from filing yet another lawsuit against us a few months later).

---

7   President of the right-wing National Front party

The condemnation was too broad to suit the tastes of a handful of journalists, sociologists, members of the Party of Colonial Peoples of the Republic, and the Collective Against Racism and Islamophobia.

Their statement begins thus: "We affirm that a Molotov cocktail hurled by night into deserted offices, and causing only material damage, does not deserve greater media and political attention than the very reticent coverage accorded to the burning or sacking of a mosque or a Muslim cemetery." How do you respond to something like that? These fine folk are basically exactly right. Let me just clarify the facts a bit: the fire was started by two incendiary devices on the same day that *Charlie Hebdo*'s website was pirated by an Islamist Turk and the staff received a raft of death threats.

The problem with their statement of outrage is its title, which implies that support for *Charlie Hebdo* somehow represents opposition to freedom of expression. Clearly, not all those who expressed their support for *Charlie Hebdo* agreed with the newspaper's editorial perspective, but all had rallied behind an independent journalistic publication that had been attacked in a more or less democratic country. They were defending not *Charlie Hebdo* but the very principle of free expression. Of course, mosques are well-known havens for freedom of expression, and Muslim cemeteries are hotbeds of debate on major current issues. *Charlie Hebdo* was guilty of being neither a mosque nor a Muslim cemetery.

The appeal continues: "There is one aspect of free expression that is indeed truly threatened—that of women, for instance, who wish to dress as they see fit, without a secular nation-state imposing a dress code that forces good Muslim women to loose their hair to the wind." The document goes on to champion the homeless, the unemployed, the working poor, and the "perpetual also-rans in the official public arena." The petitioners needed a pinch of social agenda to make it easier to swallow this indigestible stew, in which one person's liberty is assumed to cancel out someone else's. It would not, unfortunately, mask the taste of propagandist Islamist hogwash.

This valiant team of Zorros for Islam, while rightly critiquing the mainstream press, failed to note that the latter gives far more coverage to the abuse of veiled women on the street than to newspaper vendors who are threatened because they sell *Charlie Hebdo*. Let them rest assured that, in a country where news vendors prefer to hide their copies of *Charlie Hebdo* rather than be harassed for trying to sell them, their vision of free expression is on the verge of triumph.

Top billing

On a different tack, let's not forget al-Qaeda. Or to be precise, al-Qaeda in the Arabian Peninsula, which since 2010 has published a magazine for young Western militants, *Inspire,* online and in English. It was in this magazine that the two young Chechens who committed the Boston bombing attack of April 15, 2013, found the recipe for their explosives. The magazine does not limit itself to inciting Muslim simpletons of the West to murder infidels; it also offers practical advice. Take a few planks, stud them with a bunch of long nails, and head for the nearest highway overpass. Chuck your handiwork onto the road, stand back, and admire the results: heaps of scrap metal and corpses in the name of Allah. You have just taken your first action for jihad. True story. The magazine has published similar pranks and tips that are too numerous to list here.

In its March 2013 edition, *Inspire* published an announcement containing the names of eleven persons accused of "crimes against Islam" and who were wanted "dead or alive." I found my name among them, misspelled but accompanied by a photo of my mug, looking terrified. It was from a press photo taken the day of the attack on *Charlie Hebdo*. Funny. I'm in good company in the announcement—sort of. There is the inescapable Salman Rushdie; Geert Wilders, leader of the extreme right in the Netherlands; Flemming Rose, culture editor of the Danish daily *Jyllands-Posten*, at whose initiative the Muhammad cartoons were published; Terry Jones, an American pastor and total nutjob who has burned Korans; and some other lucky laureates. In order to ensure that the loons who read *Inspire* understand what is expected of them, a smoking gun is pictured to the left of the Nazi pastor's head and a pool of blood to the right. This subtle montage is entitled "YES WE CAN," with a subtitle below: *"A bullet a day keeps the infidel away."* And at the bottom: "Defend Prophet Muhammad peace be upon him."

The struggle against Islamophobia can be waged in many different ways (I far prefer the half-baked efforts of Karim Achoui, even if *Inspire* does comedy better), but the goal is always the same: to prevent the infidel from blaspheming. Yes, I know, it's disingenuous to put citizens who take us to court and criminals who threaten us with death on the same footing. But if my hyperbole can make those who call *Charlie Hebdo* a racist newspaper see how easy it is to make shameful comparisons, it will not have been in vain.

Freedom of expression and the butterfly effect

Here's another argument that has been made against the freedom of expression practiced by the artists of *Charlie Hebdo:* Through the magic of social networking, the drawings you publish in your newspaper, which sells a bare handful of copies in France, will be seen by millions of Muslim web surfers. When a little drawing beats its wings here, it unleashes a shitstorm of hatred on the other side of the world. You must remember that, in this day and age, whenever you express yourself, like it or not you are speaking to the entire planet. You need to be careful. You have to act *responsibly.*

Respect raised to the level of first principle

On a visit to Cairo in September 2012, Prime Minister Jean-Marc Ayrault and Minister for Foreign Affairs Laurent Fabius described *Charlie Hebdo* as "irresponsible" because several of our drawings had addressed the grotesque Internet-based film *Innocence of Muslims,* which I already mentioned, and the angry demonstrations it had provoked in the "Muslim world." Following their lead, many political and religious dignitaries denounced *Charlie Hebdo's* irresponsibility. Making fun of such a wretched movie, of the disproportionate reaction of a handful of angry Muslims, and of the media saturation around it—and all with a few strokes of a pencil published in a French newspaper sold exclusively at newsstands—was "adding fuel to the fire."

The television networks aired interviews with French expatriates who blamed *Charlie Hebdo* for the threats directed at them and their families. Security for French embassies in so-called Muslim countries was beefed up, and French schools overseas were closed for a few days.

Charlie Hebdo had become more dangerous than al-Qaeda. Better yet, *Charlie Hebdo* justified the existence of terrorist groups claiming to be Islamic. Drawings hastily condemned as Islamophobic legitimized the activities of murderers. *Charlie Hebdo* had acted provocatively; it was only natural to anticipate a violent reaction.

The newspaper, which does its best to adhere to French press law, had suddenly been enjoined, including by French government ministers, to respect unwritten international laws promulgated by a few purportedly Muslim wackos. What conclusions are to be drawn from these events? That we have to cave to pressure exerted by terrorists? That French law should conform with sharia? But with which version? Clearly, the strictest. It's less risky.

If tomorrow some terrorist claiming to be a Buddhist wreaks havoc on the planet, we will be asked above all not to portray the instigators of such violence for fear of stirring up the fury of Buddhists the world over. And if the next day a vegetarian terrorist threatens to kill anyone who dares assert that our taste buds delight in meat, we will be required to respect the carrot just as we are required to respect the brotherhood of prophets of the three monotheistic religions.

We are asked to respect Islam, but respecting Islam is not the same as fearing it, even if there's no crime in fearing it. There is no respect for Islam in conflating it with Islamic terrorism.

The people who start howling the minute *Charlie Hebdo* publishes a drawing of a self-styled Islamic terrorist toe a particular line. They suggest that by caricaturing an Islamist terrorist, the cartoonist is really symbolizing all Muslims. So long as the terrorist is identifiable as a Muslim, the cartoonist must be mocking all Islam. If you draw a jihadist doing what jihadists do, you are dragging the billions of faithful through the mud. If you draw Muhammad denouncing the extremists among his followers, you're insulting all Muslims. The terrorist must be stripped of any element that could identify him as a Muslim, while it is quite simply forbidden to represent Muhammad at all. If portraying an Islamist terrorist as grotesque is Islamophobic, that's the same as saying that all Muslims are terrorists or sympathetic to terrorists.

Those who accuse *Charlie Hebdo*'s artists of Islamophobia every time one of their characters sports a beard are not only dishonest or of gratuitous bad faith, but they are also revealing their support for so-called radical Islam. When you draw an old man engaged in pedophilia, you are not casting aspersions on all old men or suggesting that all old men are pedophiles (or vice-versa), and other than a rare few idiots, no one would accuse the cartoonists of *Charlie Hebdo* of that. The drawing is just an old pedophile, nothing more.

The front page of the 2006 *Charlie Hebdo* issue featuring the Danish cartoons and signed by Cabu is a perfect example. A bearded fellow in a turban holds his head in his hands. He is either fuming or weeping—perhaps both. In a speech bubble, he says: "It's hard to be loved by assholes…" The title above the drawing explains: "Muhammad fed up with the fundamentalists." The drawing explicitly shows Muhammad complaining about the attitude of fundamentalists, yet *Charlie Hebdo* was virulently criticized for suggesting that all those who worship the prophet of Islam are assholes. The cartoons in *Charlie Hebdo* are not merely misinterpreted by illiterates, but deliberately twisted by wise guys to distort their meaning.

Since, by their lights, *Charlie Hebdo* is an Islamophobic newspaper, and therefore racist, our detractors sometimes alter a drawing to make it conform to their conception of the publication. A drawing from October 2013 made the rounds of social media. Signed by Charb, it depicted the head of Minister of Justice Christiane Taubira on the body of a monkey. The drawing was indeed mine, but it had been stripped of its essentials. I'd made it to denounce the attitude of a National Front candidate in the municipal elections who had attached a monkey's body to the Minister's face in a photo on his Facebook page; I'd called it "Rassemblement Bleu Raciste,"[8] and included the National Front's tricolor flame emblem at the bottom left. These two identifying markers had been removed from my parody of the National Front poster. By

---

8   A pun on the Rassemblement Bleu Marine, a coalition of right-wing parties led by National Front President Marine Le Pen

whom? The first person to distribute the drawing without its text and flame was the singer Disiz, in 2013.

Disiz had contributed to a rap song that had been used to promote the launch of a film called *La Marche,* which was strongly inspired by the 1983 March for Equality and Against Racism. Thirteen rappers had collaborated in writing the song, including Akhenaton, Kool Shen, Soprano, and Nekfeu. The latter had composed the following verses: "There's no one lamer than a racist / These theorists want to silence Islam / What's the real danger: terrorism or Taylorism?[9] / My boys get up early,[10] I've seen them hustle / I call for a public burning for those dogs at *Charlie Hebdo.*"

Charlie Hebdo had been firebombed in 2011 after it published an issue entitled "Charia Hebdo" to lam-

---

9   Theory of workflow management invented by Frederick Winslow Taylor

10 This refers to a phrase Nicolas Sarkozy used in the 2007 presidential campaign, in which he claimed to represent French people who want to "work more to earn more" and must therefore "get up early." Having become something of a slogan, this phrase is now often used ironically to criticize Sarkozy's politics.

poon the possible establishment of sharia law in Tunisia and Libya. Nekfeu's poetic invitation was thus a call for a second arson attack on the newspaper for religious reasons. *Charlie Hebdo* responded to Nekfeu, but it was Disiz who retorted by posting the doctored drawing on Instagram, claiming that *Charlie Hebdo*, a rag well known for its Islamophobia, was also racist. Disiz concluded his polemic with a charming warning, again on Instagram, to the cartoonists at *Charlie Hebdo*: "Even if you were mutes I'd silence your voices. Wanna know how I'd do it? Well, I'd cut off your hands…"

Something similar happened with a former *Charlie Hebdo* colleague who now makes his living denouncing the newspaper's racism (which obviously started the day he left) with remarkable bad faith. He, too, has found it useful to back up his statements by publishing drawings completely out of context. For instance, a drawing of a particularly nutty (but real) Belgian Islamist, about whom a *Charlie* reporter had written a lengthy exposé, was reprinted without the accompanying text and denounced as representing the "typical Muslim."

What's in it for people who seem to be sincere in their fight against racism to hold *Charlie Hebdo* up as a racist publication? A newspaper that champions voting rights for immigrants, legal status for the un-documented, anti-racist legislation... Shouldn't we be on the same side? Yes. But that would be forgetting that it's not the struggle against racism these folks are really interested in; it's the promotion of Islam.

Caution and cowardice promoting Islamophobia

Happily, not everyone is as reckless as *Charlie Hebdo* when faced with the threat of being fingered as an Islamophobe or blasphemer. For instance, the 2012 celebration of the contemporary arts festival in Toulouse known as Springtime in September: Moroc-can artist Mounir Fatmi presented his work *Technolo-gia,* a video projection on the Pont-Neuf that included verses from the Koran. Because "sacred texts," Koranic suras, had been projected (accidentally, it turns out) on the pavement of the Pont-Neuf, a tiny group of self-styled Muslims protested on the pretext that it was an insult to their religion to trample underfoot verses of the sacred text. A passerby was punched for having walked over them. An imam was called in to restore calm, and a dozen police cars took up positions at the perimeter of the sacrilege.

The artist was dumbfounded. "This project, an homage to my Arab-Muslim heritage that has been purchased and presented by the Arab Museum of Modern Art in Doha, Qatar, has never had any problems until today." After an emergency meeting at city hall, attended by Muslim representatives, the artist decided to call it quits. "As the appropriate conditions for the exhibition of my piece are not in place, thereby preventing it from being interpreted and, above all, understood, I prefer to shelve it." At the same time, Paul Ardenne, the director of Springtime in September, was cowering in his boots: "In the current, hypersensitive context, it's better this way."

In caving to an extremist minority that represents

no one but itself, you acknowledge its power. These radicals co-opt the voice of Islam, and everyone pretends they are right. It would seem that in France, then, Islam is no longer embodied in its millions of adherents who are a pain in no one's ass, whether they practice their religion or not, but is officially represented by a handful of loudmouths. And it's not Muslims who are to blame for this, but a bunch of overfed middle-class morons terrified by the very idea of Muslims and, naturally, deeply intolerant of and highly sensitive to any speech or act that might be interpreted as Islamophobic.

What do the work of Mounir Fatmi and the cartoons of *Charlie* have in common? The outrage of a few dipshits.

Eminent, terrorized intellectuals, moralizing old clowns, and half-witted journalists have, in all earnestness, openly questioned whether it was wise to publish the cartoons of Muhammad "in the current environment." In Toulouse, a work of art that in no way contravened the rules of Islam was canceled because it was potentially Islamophobic. The time for debating the limits of freedom of expression has passed. The time for discussing whether such or such drawing is in good taste or bad has passed. The censors no longer want anything to do with this whore called free expression. No discussion whatsoever! But they're right to flaunt their barbarous stupidity, since it works. Self-censorship is becoming a major art form in France.

Mounir Fatmi was afraid that his work would not be understood—but by whom? Those blowhards will never understand anything; there's nothing to explain! So long as the biggest jerk in the Taliban is unable to understand my art, I refuse to express myself—is that it? The Koran is not only the holy book of the Muslims; it is also simply a (copyright-free) book and thus the heritage of all humankind.

To suggest that only the imams and faithful are permitted to mention the Koran, the prophet, or God without lapsing into Islamophobia is to play right into the hands of the most radical Islamists. And in giving credence only to the voices of extremists, we are doing nothing but creating hatred of Islam.

Toward the definition of a promising concept

Jealous Catholics

The term "Islamophobia" has become so popular that the Catholic extreme right, which sees Islam as both a "false religion" and as intolerable competition, has tried to co-opt the idea. In demonstrations against certain theatrical productions that have presented Jesus in a manner contrary to canon law, as well as in marches against marriage equality, chants have been heard denouncing "Cathophobia." Just as there are

Islamophobia and Islamophobes, why shouldn't there also be Cathophobia and Cathophobes? Having very frequently published images of Jesus, the Pope, the saints, and the whole gamut of liturgical paraphernalia, *Charlie Hebdo* has been sued a good dozen times by the General Alliance against Racism and for Respect of French and Christian Identity (AGRIF), an organization of Catholic fundamentalists who long maintained close ties with the National Front.

AGRIF fights racism...anti-white and anti-Christian racism. It has accused *Charlie Hebdo* of anti-French racism, among other things. How do Catholic fundamentalists define anti-French racism? Easy. By depicting the Holy Virgin in positions described nowhere in her official biography, we insult France. Indeed, ever since Louis XIII consecrated his person and his country to the Mother of God, France and the Virgin have been indivisible. To make fun of the Virgin is to make fun of France and all the French.

That was before the invention of Islamophobia. Today, the artists and editors of *Charlie Hebdo* are not so much anti-French racists as they are Cathophobes. If it works for Muslims, there's no reason it shouldn't work for Catholics and, more broadly, for Christians. Yes, Christianophobia is a scourge besetting the "eldest daughter of the Church" (but not exactly, since it was not the Kingdom of France but the Kingdom of Armenia that was the first to convert to Christianity).

On October 29, 2011, Catholic fundamentalists from the organization Civitas concluded their national demonstration against Christianophobia in front of the Théâtre de la Ville, in Paris, to protest the production of the Romeo Castellucci play *On the Concept of the Face, Regarding the Son of God,* which they considered to be blasphemous. They were joined in solidarity by a small group of Muslims. It was a blast to see (I was there) the many Catholics of Civitas chanting "Hail Mary, full of grace" on their knees amid clouds of teargas to the left of the theater, while across the street, on the traffic island in the place du Châtelet, bearded men egged them on with banners printed with such slogans as "Hands Off Issa!"—"Issa" meaning Jesus in Arabic. While Muslims do not consider Jesus to be the son of God, he is nevertheless a major prophet for them.

The problem was, the Civitas militants were separated from their Muslim friends by a cordon of riot police, who prevented all contact between them. The praying Christians were seized by a vague sense of disquiet upon noticing the bearded Muslims. Many failed to understand that the Muslims were there in support of their protest and wondered aloud what those "towel-heads" were doing there. Were they hostile? No, they were not. But the sentiments expressed that day by some Catholic fundamentalists were not so much Islamophobic as out-and-out racist. Never mind. The Catholic extreme right does not need the support of Muslim fundamentalists; it only needs their vocabulary. If Islam picked up a few characters from Christianity to bolster its own legitimacy, in return, Catholic fundamentalists centuries later have picked up a few propaganda gimmicks from their Muslim counterparts.

Catholic fundamentalists await every triumph by Muslim fundamentalists in their fight against Islamophobia with both voracity and jealousy. On February 7 and 8, 2007, in the lawsuit brought against *Charlie Hebdo* by three Muslim organizations for having republished the Danish cartoons, the plaintiffs called only one witness: a Catholic priest. Could be an alliance in the making.

Catholic fundamentalists, as well as others reputed to be more moderate, have been sulking since 1905 over the adoption of the law separating church and state and dreaming of their revenge. What jurisprudence delivers to Muslims, it could deliver equally to other believers.

The terms "Cathophobic" and "Christianophobic" have yet to achieve the media success enjoyed by "Islamophobic" because there is a real difference between anti-Muslim acts and those seen as anti-Christian. There are far more anti-Muslim acts, even though there are fewer Muslims than Christians in France, and there's not much evidence of discrimination against Christians because of their religious beliefs. But there's no reason to despair; if you rehash a lie often enough, it ends up becoming the truth.

What about Judeophobia?

All that's missing are Jewish fundamentalists to complete the circle. There is indeed such a thing as "Judeophobia," but the term is highly ambiguous. It's not clear whether it connotes hatred of the Jew who is born of Jewish parents, who belongs to Jewish culture and the Jewish people; or the Jew who is an adherent of the Jewish religion. Yes, Jewish people / Jews are a pain. They only have one word for two distinct things. Just as not all Arabs are Muslims and not all Europeans are Christians, not all Jewish people are Jews. So how the hell do you poke fun at Jewish religious extremists without conflating them with the Jewish people as a whole? By depicting them precisely. It's not that complicated. No more complicated than distinguishing between jihadist and Muslim, Muslim and immigrant, Muslim and Arab, Arab and North African, and so on.

But the grand plan of the enemies of Islamophobia is to place anti-Semitism and criticism of anyone who claims to follow Islam on the same footing. Making fun of an Islamist terrorist would be the same as insisting that Jews are inferior or noxious beings. The Internet is infested with commentary insinuating that the liberties cartoonists take with Muslims (and I repeat, drawing a Muslim with a Kalashnikov doesn't mean that all Muslims carry them), they would never dare take with Jews. Well, exactly. Not if we're talking about the Jewish people. Just as you wouldn't ridicule the Arab people because they are Arabs, you wouldn't ridicule the Jewish people for being Jewish.

On the other hand, we certainly do equate Jewish religious extremists who, for instance, stalk Palestinians in the West Bank by bulldozer and machine gun with jihadists who stalk infidels in Iraq or Syria. We don't draw an Arab in Muslim dress if we want to represent an Arab, and we don't draw a Jew in a rabbi's clothes if we want to represent a Jew. There is no correspondence between racism or anti-Semitism and the critique of religious extremists. But the inventors of Islamophobia won't budge; they absolutely insist that Islamophobia be treated as anti-Muslim racism equivalent to anti-Semitism, which is anti-Jewish racism.

And idiots aren't the only ones preaching in favor of this recognition. On September 20, 2012, the admirable reporter Alain Gresh published a lengthy article in *Le Monde diplomatique* in which he excoriated

Charlie Hebdo for its "irresponsibility." According to him, *Charlie Hebdo,* a liberal, anti-racist publication, was playing into the hands of the right and extreme right. He wrote, in part:

> Let's imagine that it's 1931 in Germany. Just as anti-Semitism is really beginning to take off, a leftist weekly issues a special edition on Judaism (the religion) in which it demonstrates at great length, without the least connotation of anti-Semitism, that Judaism is backwards, that the Bible is an apologia for violence, genocide, and stoning, that religious Jews wear funny clothes and conspicuous religious symbols, etc. It would obviously be impossible to dissociate such a publication from the German political context and the rise of Nazism....In Europe we are seeing the rise of nationalist forces and parties whose principal weapon is no longer anti-Semitism, as it was in the 1930s, but Islamophobia.

Charlie Hebdo might indeed have said all this about Judaism (the religion), with the caveat that we would have been talking about Jewish religious extremists and not about all practicing Jews. But was there an international terrorist movement in 1931 that claimed to act on behalf of Orthodox Judaism? Were there Jewish jihadists threatening to establish the equivalent of sharia law in Libya, Tunisia, Syria, and Iraq? Did Rabbi Bin Laden send a biplane crashing into the Empire State Building? I'm no historian, but I don't think so. Jewish fundamentalism was not to 1931 what Muslim fundamentalism is to the twenty-first century. And no, Islamophobia is not the new anti-Semitism. There is no new anti-Semitism, only racism—ancient, disgusting, and immortal. Racism that victimizes people of Muslim origin, for sure. Today, in France, the most violent racism is directed against the Romas. Do we need to call it "Romaphobia?" Don't be stupid. It's racism directed against the Roma.

Why this grim determination to pair anti-Semitism with Islamophobia? The only outcome of such an association would be to make the word "racism" obsolete.

· · ·

On March 16, 2007, long before Alain Gresh wrote his article, Plantu, our fellow cartoonist at *Le Monde,* who was deeply involved in the campaign against censorship, was invited to a debate convened by the UN in Geneva. There, as reported by Agence France-Presse, he called for a "blasphemy ceasefire." According to Plantu, the ceasefire would have to be equally respected by "Middle Eastern artists who draw Jews or Israelis with hook noses." Reading statements like this, you have to kind of hang your head and wonder if it's time to change jobs. For Plantu, it would seem, criticizing religion is the equivalent of racism. Plantu equates cartoonists who draw Muhammad with those who participated in the Holocaust drawing contest[11] organized by Iran at around the same time. In Plantu's opinion, Middle Eastern artists confuse anti-Semitism with blasphemy; two can play at that game by claiming that the Holocaust is a religion and for that very reason its occurrence cannot be denied. And while we're at it, why not say that there is just as

---

11   The official name reported in the media was the International Holocaust Cartoon Contest.

much evidence of the existence of God as there is of the occurrence of the Holocaust. That sound you hear? It's the Holocaust deniers rubbing their hands together in gleeful anticipation.

There's no such thing as anti-republican blasphemy!

Sadly, the religious propagandists seeking to make blasphemy a crime in France are not alone. The state itself sometimes sets a bad example. While the word "blasphemy" does not appear in the statutes, and neither do "Francophobia" or "republicophobia," there are laws that criminalize and punish anti-republican or anti-French blasphemy.

In protest against the decree of July 21, 2010, which outlawed the desecration of the French flag, and against the law of March 18, 2003, which outlawed any public affront to the national anthem or the tricolor flag, in January 2011 *Charlie Hebdo* called on the citizenry to rise up against censorship. We asked them to ridicule, destroy, or soil the symbol of the Republic. This was an invitation not to destroy anyone's property, but to demonstrate that a secular republic may not decide for its citizens which symbols are sacred and which are not.

I recall that on March 6, 2010, the Nice branch of the retail chain Fnac held an amateur photography contest. To illustrate the theme "politically incorrect," one contestant took a picture of a man wiping his ass with the tricolor flag. The photo was honored by the jury and published in the March 19 edition of the free handout *Metro*. The Police Commissioner, the President of the right-wing UMP party, the General Council, and veterans' organizations protested. Attorney General Michèle Alliot-Marie and Minister of the Interior Brice Hortefeux also expressed their righteous indignation.

On May 25, 2010, Louis Nègre, the UMP[12] senator for Alpes-Maritime, announced that he had filed a bill that would criminalize the desecration of national emblems. On July 1, 2010, it was reported in the press that two Fnac executives had received notices of ter-

---

12   Union pour un mouvement populaire was at the time the center-right party of Nicolas Sarkozy. He has since founded a new party called Les Républicains.

mination for grave misconduct. According to company management, they were charged with having "validated" the scandalous outcome of the photography competition.

On July 23, 2010, the decree outlawing desecration of the flag was published in the government gazette:

Desecration of the tricolor flag

Art. R. 645-15. Other than cases stipulated in article 433-5-1, the following acts are punishable by fine, as prescribed for misdemeanors of the fifth class, when committed in circumstances likely to lead to a disturbance of the public order and with the intention of desecrating the tricolor flag:

1) To destroy, damage, or handle the flag in a demeaning manner in a public place or one accessible to the public;

2) For the author of such acts, even when committed in private, to distribute or cause to be distributed recorded images of their commission.

3) A second offense of the misdemeanors herein proscribed shall be sanctioned pursuant to articles 132-11 and 132-15.

On September 27, 2010, the Human Rights League announced that it had filed an appeal against the decree with the Council of State. The League believed that the decree was "a violation of the Constitution and of the principle of freedom of expression." The League apparently never received a response.

On December 22, 2010, for the first time, a man was found guilty of desecration of the French flag under the terms of the decree. A first offense was not too costly—Mr. Saïdi was given a suspended €750 fine for having broken a flagpole bearing the tricolor flag at the prefecture, the provincial government headquarters in Nice. The previous day, Mr. Saïdi, an Algerian who had gone there to renew his working papers, blew a gasket when he was asked once again to come back another time. He grabbed the flagpole set up in the lobby, snapped it in two, and threw it at the functionary, missing him. Two police officers subdued him—with some difficulty, it would seem.

The Alpes-Maritime prefecture logically charged him with "destruction of public property and damage to a symbol of the French Republic." Since it was now allowed to do so, it threw in the charge of "desecration of the tricolor flag." The functionaries involved also filed charges. And Mr. Saïdi, in addition to being found guilty of desecration, copped a four-month suspended jail sentence for insurrection.

Was the flag desecration decree necessary to bring the hothead to justice? Clearly not. Damage to public property and insurrection would have sufficed. But in the atmosphere that had been deliberately created by the government of the time by promoting a debate on national identity, the opportunity to prosecute a foreigner—better yet, an Algerian—for desecration was too good to pass up. The prefecture, an instrument of the discriminatory policies of the Sarkozian state, needed to test out this new weapon, which will also be used sooner or later against naughty French citizens.

Funny, no one was outraged when the National Front co-opted the national colors for its logo. My blaspheming friends, you'd better act quick if you want to have your fun. In the stunted, fearful, sclerotic, mean-spirited, and bitter France of today, pissing on the flame logo of the National Front will soon be designated a desecration of the flag and cost you €1,500.

Charlie Hebdo has never been charged under the law criminalizing the desecration of the flag. It would appear that the law has not been applied since the Saïdi affair, but it's still on the books and the reactionaries will resort to it one of these days, since there's no law preventing them from running for office and getting elected. Come to think of it, apparently, it's not showing a lack of respect for the Republic to risk putting the keys to the Élysée palace in the pudgy hands of the extreme right.

Here's another, equally absurd illustration of the campaign to recognize republican blasphemy, modeled on religious blasphemy.

On September 17, 2010, four Islamists dressed in black are haranguing a crowd in central Limoges. One of the men has a megaphone, while two of his pals hold up a black banner on which the profession of the

Muslim faith is inscribed in white Arabic script. The speaker, sporting a beard and a white skullcap, brandishes a copy of the French Penal Code while denouncing its "3,000 pages," which supposedly protect individual rights. And yet, among these 3,000 pages, "not one line protects the rights of Muslims." "In France, you have the right to be Islamophobic," he concludes, outraged, as he hurls the Penal Code to the ground. "Since the book doesn't protect us, we will not respect it. Until it has been amended, this book, and no other, deserves to be burned!" Rather than burn it, he kicks it away. The event was recorded, and the video is surely still hanging around somewhere on YouTube.

What became of the firebrand? His name is Mohamed Achamlane, and he was the leader of a tiny Islamist group calling itself Forsane Alizza—the Knights of Pride—that was dissolved in February 2012. He committed acts far worse than throwing books on the ground, and was brought to justice. But for his lack of respect for the Penal Code, as well as for leading an invasion of a McDonald's restaurant on June 12, 2010, and calling for a boycott of the chain, which he accuses of supporting Israel, he was found guilty on June 9, 2011, of "public incitement to national, racial, or religious discrimination." He was given a four-month suspended sentence and a €2,000 fine. To be sure, his conviction was not based exclusively on the act of throwing the Penal Code to the ground, but he was also found guilty of that crime, although no one could quite identify the statute criminalizing blasphemy against the Penal Code.

Honestly, how can anyone be convicted for kicking a book, whatever kind of book it may be? Whether it's the Koran, the Bible, the Torah, the Penal Code, a Codes Rousseau guidebook for student drivers, the Yellow Pages, or even the second volume of the adventures of Valérie Trierweiler,[13] it's only a few sheets of paper stained with ink. It's particularly moronic to burn a book, but sanctifying symbols—be they republican, religious, or other—is not an especially sound practice either.

In October 2010, a resident of Bischheim, in the department of Bas-Rhin, filmed himself making paper

---

13   Former partner of French President François Hollande

planes from pages torn from the Koran, then launching them toward glasses intended to represent the towers of the World Trade Center. For his final act, he burned what remained of the Koran and then urinated on it to extinguish the flames. The author posted the video on the Internet. He, too, was prosecuted for public incitement to national, racial, or religious discrimination. He was found not guilty, the court having determined that the video did not go beyond "the limits on freedom of expression" and that the author had vilified "terrorist acts that cannot be attributed to the Muslim community." Phew.

If the legal system is able to distinguish between Muslims and terrorists who claim to follow Islam, why are the majority of anti-Islamophobes unable to do likewise? By the same token, it would be nice if the French legal system could see that when a French flag is burned or soiled, it is not all of France that is being impeached. And even if it were, for pity's sake let's stop persecuting blasphemers!

And what about atheophobia in all this?

If "atheophobia" denotes the violent criticism of atheism, I invite my Bible-thumping friends to sign up without fear for their safety. Don't reserve your insults to Reason for the privacy of those tombs of thought you call temples, churches, synagogues, and mosques! Publish newspapers and blogs, stage plays and puppet shows, to mock what you see as the absurdity of life without God, of life without your Supreme Blankie! Draw cartoons of the absence of God, give it a big nose, a little nose, wild eyes, shaggy hair—no atheist will sue you, you will receive no death threats, and your offices will not be destroyed.

It turns out that there is no such thing as atheist terrorism in the twenty-first century. Atheists are persecuted pretty much all over the world, but none of them destroy the works of art created by believers to honor their God. Better yet, these atheist fools are often the very first to demand protection for religious sites threatened by pious barbarians who think beauty represents blasphemy against their Creator. A Creator who is blind and deaf, mean as fuck and dumb as a plank.

Go ahead! I dare you! I dare you simply to laugh at those you consider your enemies, laugh your heart out (unless that's a sin) at the heretics, infidels, and apostates—no one will kill you in the name of something that doesn't exist! No atheist will call you an anti-atheist racist. Aren't atheists cool? Atheists will rouse themselves to seek justice only when they are the victims of discrimination based on their lack of faith. Refusing to hire an atheist because he's an atheist and refusing to hire a Muslim because he's Muslim are covered by the same laws, the same rights, the same courts. No form of discrimination is better or worse than any other.

About the Author

Charb (Stéphane Charbonnier, August 21, 1967–January 7, 2015) was a French journalist, political cartoonist, and satirist. Born and raised outside of Paris, Charb honed his drawing skills as a teenager and contributed illustrations to his college newspaper and local publications. He joined the staff of *Charlie Hebdo* in 1992 and held the position of editor in chief from 2009 until his death in 2015. An atheist, pacifist, and staunch advocate of free speech, Charb was known for cartoons that mocked political figures and organized religion.